Death, Hell, and The Resurrection

Vincent Padgett

TEACH Services, Inc.
PUBLISHING
www.TEACHServices.com • (800) 367-1844

This book was written to provide truthful information in regard to the
subject matter covered. The author assumes full responsibility
for the accuracy of all facts and quotations as cited in this book.
The opinions expressed in this book are the author's personal
views and interpretation of the Bible, Spirit of Prophecy,
and/or contemporary authors and do not necessarily
reflect those of TEACH Services, Inc.

This book is sold with the understanding that the publisher is not engaged
in giving spiritual, legal, medical, or other professional advice.
If authoritative advice is needed, the reader should
seek the counsel of a competent professional

———————————————

Copyright © 2013 TEACH Services, Inc.
ISBN-13: 978-1-4796-0044-1 (Paperback)
ISBN-13: 978-1-4796-0045-8 (ePub)
ISBN-13:978-1-4796-0046-5 (Kindle / Mobi)

Published by

TEACH Services, Inc.
P U B L I S H I N G
www.TEACHServices.com ● (800) 367-1844

Table of Contents

Introduction

The resurrection and what happens when people die is a subject comprised of the following three questions: (1) what happens to people when they die (i.e. their "soul" and their body); (2) what happens to the "saved" and the "lost"; is there more than one resurrection; and (3) what is heaven and hell?

The Bible alone should be used to answer these questions, and it is the intent to do so in this book while refraining from the philosophy and ideas of men. Where necessary quotes from historians or theologians may be used to show the origin of false teachings that are contrary to the Bible.

As little explanation as possible of Bible verses will be used because God's Word speaks for itself and requires no lengthy, elaborate translation: "At that time Jesus answered and said, I thank thee, O Father, Lord of heaven and earth, because thou hast hid these things from the wise and prudent, and hast revealed them unto babes" (Matt. 11:25). Any doctrine that requires long, interpretative explanations should be a sign of warning.

This study is so important because Christianity rests upon this one point—the resurrection. "Now if Christ be preached that he rose from the dead, how say some among you that there is no resurrection of the dead? But if there be no resurrection of the dead, then is Christ not risen: and if Christ be not risen, then is our preaching vain, and your faith is also vain. Yea, and we are found false witnesses of God; because we have testified of God that he raised up Christ … But now is Christ risen from the dead, and become the firstfruits of them that slept" (1 Cor. 15:12–20).

Notice the word firstfruits. Christ is the first of many who will be raised from the dead. Also notice that the apostle Paul calls death a sleep, an interesting description of death that proves significant when the same writer calls death by the name of "death" elsewhere.

I invited you to take an honest look at what the Bible says about Christ's resurrection, His second coming, the judgment of every human beings, the resurrection of the saved and the lost, and heaven and hell. May God lead you into all truth.

Chapter 1

A History of Christ's Resurrection

Two historical facts deserve mention here. When researching ancient documents of those who denied Christ, we find many admissions that Jesus was a real person who did great miracles, who died, and whom many thousands quickly believed had risen from the dead, but they leave it at that. On the other hand, there are eyewitness accounts of those claiming to have seen Jesus' resurrection, but many of these people were martyred for their preaching.

As we read in 1 Corinthians 15:12–20, Paul claimed to be an eyewitness to a risen Savior. But there were many more witnesses over a period of forty days (Acts 1:3): the twelve disciples (Mark 16:12, 14), some specific women followers (Luke 24:10), and more than 500 others (1 Corinthians 15:5). That some of the eyewitnesses wrote the books of the New Testament and other books is irrefutable as can easily be proven through research.

History documents that people have died for erroneous beliefs, but never has anyone or a group of people died for something they *knew* to be a lie. Cornelius Tacitus, a Roman historian, wrote that the Christians had total disregard for their very lives. They *knew* they would live again. They had the assurance they were not dying in vain. What power had death?

To understand the history surrounding Christ's death, let's look at the writings of Tacitus (AD 55–120). Some of his famous works are the *Annals*, covering Augustine's death (AD 14) to that of Nero (AD 68), and the *Histories*, from Nero's death to Domitian (AD 96).

While writing about Nero, Tacitus states, "But not all the relief that could come from man, not all the bounties that the prince could bestow nor all the atonements which could be presented to the gods, availed to relieve Nero from the infamy of being believed to have ordered the conflagration, the fire of Rome. Hence to suppress the rumor, he falsely charged with the guilt, and punished with the most exquisite tortures, the persons commonly called Christians, who were hated for their enormities. Christus [a misspelling of Christ] the founder of the name was put to death by Pontius Pilate, procurator of Judea in the reign of Tiberius: but the pernicious superstition, repressed for a time, broke out again, not only through Judea, where the mischief originated, but through the city of Rome also" (*Annals*, XV, p. 44).

The "pernicious," or mischievous, superstition is what non-Christians called the belief in Christ's resurrection. Also, Pilate is mentioned here, confirming the account of the Bible along with the reign of Tiberius, which fixes the date of Christ's crucifixion to AD 31. All this proves that Jesus, in fact, existed and died under a Roman administered death penalty. Tacitus was irrefutably a pagan, yet he clearly wrote about Jesus. There's no use denying that non-Christians wrote about Him. Just as interesting, no one during this era wrote a refutation to these writings—no one attempted to deny Christ's existence until several hundred years later.

Lucian of Samosata was a Greek satirist who mentioned the Christian's belief in immortality: "The Christians, you know, worship a man to this day—the distinguished personage who introduced their novel rites, and was crucified on that account.... You see, these misguided creatures start with the general conviction that they are immortal for all time, which explains the contempt of death and voluntary self-devotion which are so common among them; and then it was impressed on them by their original lawgiver that they are all brothers, from the moment that they are converted, and deny the gods of Greece, and worship the crucified sage, and live after his laws. All this they take quite on faith, with the result that they despise all worldly goods alike, regarding them merely as common property" (*The Death of Peregrine*, pp. 11–13).

Suetonius: Roman historian and court official under Hadrian, and Annalist of the Imperial House: "As the Jews were making constant disturbances at the instigation of Chrestus [another misspelling of Christ], he [Claudius] expelled them from Rome" (*The Life of Claudius*, p. 25.4). This occurred, by secular dating, in AD 49, which confirms the account written by Luke in Acts 18:2.

Writing about the fire in Rome in AD 64, which Tacitus confirmed in the account we just read, Suetonius pens, "Punishment by Nero was inflicted on the Christians, a class of men given to a new and mischievous superstition" (*Lives of the Caesars*, p. 16.2).

We briefly discussed that Jesus was crucified in AD 31 during the reign of Pontius Pilate, which was from AD 6–36. These writings place Christians in Rome less than twenty years after Christ's death. Eyewitnesses to Jesus' resurrection were still alive and teaching and dying for their faith, which is serious business and speaks to the magnitude of the Christian movement.

Pliny the Younger, governor of Bithynia in Asia Minor (AD 112), wrote the emperor of Trojan for advice, explaining that he had been putting to death men, women, and children who he discovered to be Christians, but so many were popping up that he needed to change his plans and maybe kill only certain ones. He said he attempted to make "them curse Christ, which a genuine Christian cannot be induced to do," but his interrogations resulted in their affirmation, "that the whole of their guilt, or their error, was that they were in the habit of meeting on a certain fixed day before it was light, when they sang in alternate verse a hymn to Christ as to a god, and bound themselves to a solemn oath, not to do any wicked deeds, but never to commit any fraud, theft, adultery, never to falsify their word, not to deny a trust when they should be called upon to deliver it up" (*Epistles*, X, p. 96).

Thallus wrote on the history of the Eastern Mediterranean world from the Trojan War to his own time. He was one of the earlier secular writers to mention Christ. His writings on Christ are dated to AD 52. His work survives only in fragments, but other historians quoted those writings as a source, and they are preserved in those later citations. One such historian was Julius Africanus (AD 221).

Africanus challenges Thallus' explanation of the darkness that fell over Jerusalem at Jesus' crucifixion. Thallus' attempt to explain it as an unnaturally long eclipse of the sun finds no support: "Thallus, in the third book of his histories, explains away this darkness as an eclipse of the sun—unreasonably, ... of course, because a solar eclipse could not take place at the time of the full moon, and it was at the season of the Paschal full moon that Christ died" (Julius Africanus, *Chronography*, p. 18.1).

Another secular historian by the name of Phlegon wrote a history called *Chronicles*. It has been lost, but was used as a reference by other historians such as Africanus, Origen, and Philopon like those of Thallus. Phlegon confirmed Africanus' assessment of the "eclipse" at Christ's death as a supernatural event.

Mara Bar-Serapion, a Syrian philosopher, in a letter to his son (circa AD 70–80) wrote, "What advantage did the Jews gain from executing their wise King? It was just after that their kingdom was abolished [AD 70].... Nor did the wise King die for good; he lived on in the teaching which He had given." Mara Bar-Serapion did not believe in Christ; he was telling his son to seek wisdom and learn from the fate of three wise men: Jesus; Socrates; and Pythagoras, who had all been put to death.

There are Jewish writings that confirm Jesus' crucifixion. The Talmud records that "on the eve of Passover Yeshua [the Hebrew name for Jesus] [was] hanged." The Jewish writings attempt to explain away Jesus' miracles as "sorcery"; thereby, affirming by non-Christians that He did perform miracles! These are official Sanhedrin documents, written by Talmudic scholars who taught against Christ. They even throw snide remarks at His virgin birth.

One such Jewish historian was Flavius Josephus. His name derives from the fact that the Flavian emperors employed him. He was a Pharisee, to boot, but he was also a traitor and backstabber. While in Rome as an "interpreter" and "mediator," he turned on his fellow rebels against Rome in the AD 66–67 revolt. He was certainly not a Christian. Among his writings are *The Jewish War* and *Antiquities of the Jews*.

"Now there was about this time Jesus, a wise man ... a doer of wonderful works ... He drew over to him both many of the Jews and many of the Gentiles.... And when Pilate, at the suggestion of the principal men amongst us, had condemned him to the cross, those that loved him at the first did not forsake him; for he appeared to them alive again the third day" (*Antiquities of the Jews*, XVIII, p. 33).

"As therefore Ananus was of such a disposition, he thought he had now a good opportunity, as Festus was now dead, and Albinus was still on the road; so he assembled a council of judges, and brought before it the brother of Jesus the so-called Christ, whose name was James [this James is the very one who wrote the book of James in the Bible], together with some others, and having accused them as lawbreakers, he delivered them over to be stoned" (Ibid., XX, p. 9.1).

Here you have an eyewitness to a risen Christ, who wrote the book of James in our Bible, being stoned. It was not safe to be a Christian after Jesus' death and resurrection.

Besides the statements by the non-Christian historians thus far, there are many early Christian writers who support our faith, but we need not go further now. It's time to move on and discuss the return of Christ.

Chapter 2

The Return of Christ

The Bible is very clear as to how Christ will return. In 1 Thessalonians we read, "For the Lord Himself shall descend from heaven with a shout, with the voice of the archangel, and with the trump of God: and the dead in Christ shall rise first: then we which are alive and remain shall be caught up together with them in the clouds, to meet the Lord in the air: and so shall we ever be with the Lord" (1 Thess. 4:16, 17).

In 1 Corinthians 15:51–54 Paul quotes from the Old Testament book of Isaiah: "Behold, I shew you a mystery; we shall not all sleep, but we shall all be changed. In a moment, in the twinkling of an eye, at the last trump: for the trumpet shall sound and the dead shall be raised incorruptible, and we shall be changed. For this corruptible must put on incorruption, and this mortal must put on immortality.... then shall be brought to pass the saying that is written Death is swallowed up in victory."

We read in the last book of the Gospels, "Marvel not at this: for the hour is coming, in the which all that are in the graves shall hear his voice, and shall come forth; they that have done good, unto the resurrection of life, and they that have done evil, unto the resurrection of damnation" (John 5:28, 29).

Isaiah speaks of that day: "Thy dead men shall live, together with my dead body shall they arise. Awake and sing, ye that dwell in dust: for thy dew is as the dew of herbs, and the earth shall cast out the dead" (Isa. 26:19).

So how many people will rise? "After this I beheld, and, lo, a great multitude, which no man could number, of all nations, and kindreds, and people, and tongues, stood before the throne, and before the Lamb" (Rev. 7:9).

Let's get a broad overview of all we're going to discuss here. First, when Jesus returns, "*every eye shall see him*" (Rev. 1:7). There is no secret resurrection, and He will not be secretly here on earth. In 1 Thessalonians 4:17 we saw that we would be "caught up together ... in the clouds, to meet the Lord in the air."

If we read the complete text in Revelation 1:7, it says, "Behold, he cometh with clouds; and *every eye shall see Him,* and they also which pierced Him." Even those who nailed Christ to the cross will see Him, including those soldiers who had a change of heart and believed on Him as their Savior and Lord.

When Jesus returned to heaven after His death, angels comforted the disciples with these words: "Ye men of Galilee, why stand ye gazing up into heaven? this same Jesus, which is taken up from you into heaven, shall so come in like manner as ye have seen him go into heaven" (Acts 1:11).

Matthew also speaks of Jesus' return in the clouds of glory. But first he warns people that false Christs and false prophets will arise (Matt. 24:24). He also tells us that Jesus will not touch the earth when He returns: "Wherefore if they shall say unto you, Behold, he is in the desert; go not forth: behold, he is in the secret chambers; believe it not." Then in verses 30 and 31, we read about His actual coming: "And then shall all the tribes of the earth mourn, and they shall see the Son of man coming in the clouds of heaven with *power* and *great glory*. And he shall send his angels with a great sound of a trumpet." Therefore, we know that His coming will be audible, and everyone will hear it.

The following verse in John 14 explains what will happen after Jesus returns. "Let not your heart be troubled: ye believe in God, believe also in me. In my Father's house are many mansions: if it were not so, I would have told you. I go to prepare a place for you. And if I go and prepare a place for you, I will come again, and receive you unto myself; that where I am, there ye may be also" (verses 1–3). It is clear that Jesus will take us to heaven when He returns. But then what?

When the righteous are taken to heaven, they are changed, putting on immortal and incorruptible bodies (1 Cor. 15:51–54). For 1,000 years the righteous are to reign in heaven.

"But the rest of the dead lived not again until the thousand years were finished. This is the *first* resurrection. Blessed and holy is he that hath part in the *first* resurrection: on such the second death hath no power" (Rev. 20:5, 6). The second death and the fact that those in Christ do not suffer this death is mentioned here. Also, the verse mentions that there is a first resurrection. Realizing this, we can deduce that there must be a second resurrection, which is also confirms by verse 5 when it declares, "the rest of the dead lived not again until the thousand years were finished."

When Jesus returns, the wicked dead are not raised and those who are not saved are destroyed by the brightness of His coming. "And then shall that Wicked be revealed, whom the Lord shall consume with the spirit of his mouth, and shall destroy with the brightness of his coming" (2 Thess. 2:8).

The earth will be desolate, a wasteland, where only Satan and his angels will wander and consider their deeds. The prophet Jeremiah foretold about this desolation: "And the slain of the Lord shall be at that day from one end of the earth even unto the other end of the earth" (Jer. 25:33). "I beheld, and, lo, the fruitful place was a wilderness, and all the cities thereof were broken down at the presence of the Lord, and by his fierce anger. For thus hath the Lord said, The whole land shall be desolate" (Jer. 4:26, 27).

Isaiah also predicted this time period: "The Lord maketh the earth empty, and maketh it waste ... the land shall be utterly emptied" (Isa. 24:1, 3). "And the slain of the Lord shall be at that day from one end of the earth unto the other end of the earth: they shall not be lamented, neither gathered, nor buried; they shall be dung upon the ground" (Jer. 25:33). There is no one left alive to even bury the dead. Those in Christ are in heaven.

After the thousand years, the wicked dead are raised and Satan gathers them together for the final deception of the wicked (Rev. 20:7, 8). But a final battle will never take place because fire will come down from heaven and destroy those who "compassed the camp of the saints" (verse 9). This verse provides us another clue that the righteous have descended from heaven and returned to earth for this final conflict.

In the next chapter, we will examine more closely the resurrection of the wicked and their destruction.

Chapter 3

The Second Death, Eternal Death, and Hell

In the last chapter we briefly touched on the subject of the "second death." The fact is that you cannot die a second death if you haven't died the first. All the wicked living are killed by "the brightness of His coming" and must then be resurrected at the end of the thousand years. Think about it, if they were not resurrected, how else could they die the second time? Please read this paragraph again and think about it very carefully. Doctrine being taught today contradicts many biblical principals such as this.

Let's turn to Revelation 20:13 and 14 to see what God's Word has to say on this subject. "And the sea gave up the dead which were in it … and they were judged every man according to their works. And death and hell were cast into the lake of fire. This is the second death." Hell comes into the picture here along with the second death. But this verse may prompt more questions than answers. How can hell be cast into the lake of fire? Then again, what is hell?

Hades is the Greek word for hell, which corresponds to the Hebrew word *sheol*, meaning grave or pit. Interestingly, although *hades* is meant to replace *sheol* in the translation into Greek, it means neither a grave nor a place, neither intermediate nor permanent. Regardless of denomination, all biblical scholars will admit, if truthful, and all language professors will tell you, the word *never* means a place. It means an "indeterminate state of death." The Bible, for this reason, consistently calls death a "sleep." Why? The state of a person's eternal consequences are "indeterminate" in this "sleep." They haven't been judged yet and found guilty or innocent. Their "state," in this respect, is undetermined. The Bible clearly supports this.

The other word used for hell, but denoting a specific place, is Gehenna. The word is used twelve times in the Bible and means "a place of burning." The word is a transliteration of the Hebrew Ge-Hinnom, which originally meant "valley of Hinnow." This valley lies southwest of Jerusalem and was a place where garbage, dead animals, and other refuse was dumped and burned.

Examining all of these words that mean hell, we find that they appear in the Bible as follows: *sheol* is used thirty-one times; *hades*, ten times; Gehenna, twelve times; and Tartarus, meaning a place of darkness, one time.

The Bible teaches that Satan and all the wicked will be completely destroyed. But will God make them burn in eternal torment for eternity as is commonly taught? Does God force people to love and worship Him because of fear of torture? As we examine Scripture, the words and their meanings do not support such a theory.

"The wages of sin is death" (Rom. 6:23). The penalty, the punishment, the "wages" of sin is not eternal life in hell or anywhere else. Eternal life is eternal life, no matter where you are. The Bible is clear that sin results in death: "Sin, when it is finished, bringeth forth death" (James 1:15); "the soul that sinneth, it shall die" (Eze. 18:20).

Now let's look at two verses in Matthew. "And fear not them which kill the body, but are not able to kill the soul: but rather fear him which is able to destroy both soul and body in hell" (Matt. 10:28). "Whose fan is in his hand, and he will thoroughly purge his floor, and gather his wheat into the garner; but he will burn up the chaff with unquenchable fire" (Matt. 3:12). The word for "up" denotes completion. Also notice the fire is unquenchable. This is important. In school, my English teachers always stressed the importance of adjectives and adverbs and their proper use. Which noun or verb do they modify? Here, it is the fire that has a quality; it is modified. I cannot overstress the importance of paying attention to details such as this, because when you examine the Bible closely, you will not find the phrase eternal torment within its pages.

"The day that cometh shall burn them up, saith the Lord of hosts, that it shall leave them neither root nor branch" (Mal. 4:1). The fire leaves *nothing*, absolutely nothing. "For they shall be ashes under the soles of your feet" (verse 3).

King David spoke about the destruction of the wicked: "For evildoers shall be *cut off* [karath in Hebrew]: but those that wait upon the Lord, they shall inherit the earth. For yet a little while, and the wicked shall not be: yea, thou shalt diligently consider his place, and it shall not be" (Ps. 37:9, 10). Karath means to "kill, destroy, consume, totally." Later on in Psalm 37:20, David penned, "But the wicked shall *perish* [avad in Hebrew], and the enemies of the Lord shall be as the fat of lambs: they shall consume; into smoke shall they consume always."

Now let's read the last part of John 3:16: "Whosoever believeth in him should not *perish* [asaph in Greek], but have everlasting life." *Asaph* is derived from the Hebrew word *avad* and means total cessation of life. There is no stronger word in that language to convey the complete end of any life. What we see above are two opposites: total cessation of life, or life without fear of that same death—eternal life versus eternal death. Those are the options. Not eternal life versus eternal life.

Turn to Isaiah 47:14: "Behold, they shall be as stubble; the fire shall burn them; they shall not deliver themselves from the power of the flame: there shall not be a coal to warm at, nor fire to sit before it." The fire goes out and leaves nothing, not even an ember.

The story of Sodom and Gomorrah helps to illustrate this truth. In writing about the end of the world, Jude said, "Even as Sodom and Gomorrha [sic] … are set forth for an example, suffering the vengeance of eternal fire" (verse 7). In light of the term eternal fire as used in Revelation, this scripture, which was written hundreds of years after those cities were destroyed by fire, seems to contradict with the idea of an "eternal" fire since Sodom and Gomorrah were not—and are not—still burning.

So what does the Bible mean when it talks about "eternal fire." Going back to English class, "fire" modifies the word "eternal." Is this word and its use defined as we define it today? The answer must be no, or the cities of Sodom and Gomorrah would still be burning today according to the writer of Jude 1:7.

So what does the word eternal mean. Based on what we've read, the word describes the fire's *effect* as being eternal. The Bible explains itself. It cannot contradict itself or the whole thing is untrustworthy. If someone teaches that a word means this here and something else there, their teaching deserves close scrutiny.

The phrase "eternal fire" is the way biblical authors and people of that era described a complete and total destruction from which nothing could arise again. This may have also been necessary from the standpoint of many pagan beliefs and myths that were being taught. One example would be the concept of a Phoenix rising from the ashes of destruction. To ensure there could be no teaching that could later twist the doctrine of Christ into a teaching where Satan and sin could arise again from the ashes and corrupt the world, this use of eternal is necessary. So the authors were illustrating the fire's eternal result.

Interestingly, a few hundred years after Christ, Christians began engaging in a very dangerous practice. Upon the tombs of martyred bishops in early Rome are carved certain symbols used in a clandestine manner to portray the belief of the one entombed there—an anchor for a cross, a fish for Jesus, and a Phoenix with a halo to signify the resurrection. Such mixture of paganism with Christianity only served to create serious problems for the temporary safety it brought.

Let's look at another example. Jeremiah 17:27 declares that Jerusalem would be destroyed with unquenchable fire, which was fulfilled in 2 Chronicles 36:19–21. The fire was unquenchable—it could not be put out until it had completed its destruction.

Jerusalem is not still burning. If you compare modern dictionaries with one from 200 years ago, you would be surprised, as I was, by the change of meanings for a variety of words. This is why it is important to understand Hebrew and Greek as it was written thousands of years ago and to understand the culture those people lived in. We wouldn't have a Chinese "scholar" immigrate to America and interpret the meaning of our ancient documents word by word without having a healthy knowledge of our history, culture, poetry, and "idioms."

Luckily for us, God is all-knowing, and He has given us a Bible that interprets itself. If we compare scripture with scripture, we will discover the answers. "Whom shall he teach knowledge?

And whom shall he make to understand doctrine? Them that are weaned from the milk, and drawn from the breasts. For precept must be upon precept, precept upon precept; line upon line, line upon line; here a little, and there a little" (Isa. 28:9, 10). If we compare scripture with scripture and harmonize them where two different interpretations can be had (because only one interpretation can be correct), then we will gain the truth. Scripture cannot contradict scripture. If one or two verses, interpreted one way, contradict several others, then we must reexamine those one or two that appear to be in contradiction with the rest.

The Bible tells us that Satan will be utterly destroyed by fire and be as if he had never existed. But he, and all the rest of the wicked, will not be left to suffer. "Thou [Satan] hast defiled thy sanctuaries by the multitude of thine iniquities, by the iniquity of thy traffick; therefore will I bring forth a fire from the midst of thee, it shall devour thee, and I will bring thee to ashes upon the earth in the sight of all them that behold thee. All they that know thee among the people shall be astonished at thee: thou shalt be a terror, *and never shalt thou be any more*" (Ezek. 28:18, 19). In Obadiah 1:16 we find similar wording about destruction: "Yea, they shall drink, and they shall swallow down, and *they shall be as though they had not been.*"

Many people do not have a correct understanding of God's character. Much confusion and resentment have been voiced over the issue of hell and God being a loving God or One of wrath. God's wrath is against sin. Few people, I suspect, can honestly say they have witnessed a heinous wrong and not been angered by it. But God's wrath is not directed at the person. He sees sin for the destructive and repulsive thing it is, and those who hold onto it will be destroyed with it. Sin cannot be allowed to rise again and bring misery to those who want eternal happiness and peace.

It is important for us to understand God's character and to represent Him in a truthful manner. God never forces worship upon anyone. Neither is acceptance of salvation forced upon anyone under fear of eternal torment. We are all slated to die. The only question remains, will we be raised to eternal life or eternal death, which is everlasting and final?

No one can be saved by fear. Salvation is a conscious choice. "But the *fearful*, and unbelieving, and the abominable, and murderers and whoremongers, and sorcerers, and idolaters, and all liars, shall have their part in the lake which burneth with fire and brimstone: which is the second death" (Rev. 21:8). The word translated as fearful here is the Greek word for "timid," meaning to not make a choice out of fear. But no choice is, in fact, a choice. We should consciously choose. When we make a conscious decision to let go of our past and turn away from sin and confess Christ as our hope, we are counted as having never done any wrong.

Fear is in opposition to faith. Romans 14:23 says, "Whatsoever is not of faith is sin." Now read 1 John 4:18: "There is no fear in love; but perfect love casteth out fear: *because fear hath torment.* He that feareth is not made perfect in love." If you are worried about the punishment of the wicked, remember this promise: "God is love" (1 John 4:8). He does not torment people. But He does give everyone a choice between everlasting life or everlasting death (1 John 4:7–16). Also, consider this, "For ye have not received the spirit of bondage again to fear; but ye have received the Spirit of adoption, whereby we cry, Abba, Father" (Rom. 8:15).

Now that we have examined the word "eternal," let's move on to the word "forever." Forever is used fifty-six times in the Bible, describing things that are already ended. One example appears in Deuteronomy 23:3 and is pointing to the tenth generations.

In the case of a person, numerous examples exist where the word simply means "as long as one lives" or "until death," those are absolute definitions given to the word by linguists of Hebrew (see also 1 Samuel 1:22, 28; Exodus 21:6; Psalm 48:14).

This is another case of understanding the meaning of words. Forever denotes a period of time until someone or something is past or gone. Forever is not associated with any specific time principle or endless time. There are phrases that will create such a time principle such as where a participle modifies the sentence. Here's an example of when the word "everlasting" takes on a meaning which is dealing with time in the sense of "never ending" or "eternal" as we know those things to mean: "even *unto* everlasting." That phrase with the word "unto" deserves special consideration.

The scriptures people cite that talk about hell fire burning forever do not list a time principle or modifier to indicate that the wicked will be tormented for eternity. Instead, when referring to hell, the word means "until death." It ends. It is final.

Chapter 4

Death a Sleep

We now need to look closely at what happens when a person dies. The Bible calls death a sleep. But where do people go when they die?

Nowhere in the Bible can we find support for the idea that a soul or spirit resides apart from the body or comes to claim it at the resurrection. Nowhere is the soul described as having any thoughts, memories, wisdom, feelings, or anything apart from the body. So what is the soul? The first mention is in Genesis 2:7. "And the Lord God formed man of the dust of the ground, and breathed into his nostrils the breath of life; *and man became a living soul.*" It doesn't say God *gave* man a soul; it says he *became* a living soul.

If it were an equation, it would look like this: Body + Breath = Soul. To use a common example: light bulb + electricity = light. Notice, electricity is unseen and has a source, just as the life is unseen and has a source. The Bible says that the breath returns to God at death, but this is not a soul. The soul is the equivalent of light in our example equation: it is life. The "breath" is sometimes translated as "spirit." Only God gives the breath, or spirit, of life. Some modern translations word the above verse so that it says that God breathed the "spirit" into man's nostrils and became—or was given—a soul. When worded this way, Adam would have both a spirit and a soul even though no scripture states any such thing.

Looking at the Old and New Testaments, it teaches that humanity is mortal and will die; that is, that the soul can and does die. The word "immortal" is used in the Bible only once, and Paul used it to describe God, not a human being (1 Tim. 1:17). And the word "immortality" is used to describe what happens to the righteous at the resurrection. *Then* and only then, we will "put on" immortality (1 Cor. 15:53, 54; Rev. 20:6).

So, if the body is in the ground, when are we judged? First, we must notice an important concept. No one is ever punished *before* being found guilty. And no one is rewarded *before* the job is completed. Let's examine the following scriptures.

"For the Son of man shall come in the glory of his Father with his angels; and *then he shall reward every man according to his works*" (Matt. 16:27).

"And I saw the dead, small and great, stand before God; and the books were opened: and another book was opened, which is the book of life: and the *dead* were judged out of those things which were written in the books, according to their works" (Rev. 20:12). This is during the thousand years when God's people are resurrected or caught up in the clouds. The righteous participate in the judgment of the wicked; there are no living judged here, as the above verse shows. The living, at this time, have already been resurrected and redeemed by Christ.

Now, how can one be judged—and punished—by going to hell and burning before the judgment? It violates the law of scripture. People don't even do that, at least in civilized societies. Is God more unjust than human beings? Revelation 22:11, 12 tells us of the reward we will receive: "He that is unjust, let him be unjust still: and he which is filthy, let him be filthy still: and he that is righteous, let him be righteous still: and he that is holy, let him be holy still. And, behold, I come quickly; and my reward is with me, to give every man according as his work shall be."

Job provides insight into the topic of death. "But man dieth, and wasteth away: yea, man giveth up the ghost [the word used here for ghost is "breath," which we discussed earlier], *and where is he?*... So man lieth down, and riseth not: till the heavens be no more, they shall not awake, nor be raised out of their sleep" (Job 14:10, 12). The heavens are "no more" when Christ returns: "And the heaven departed as a scroll when it is rolled together; and every mountain and island were moved out of their places" (Rev. 6:14).

Job also wrote, "For now shall I sleep in the dust, and thou [speaking to God] shalt seek me in the morning, but I shall not be" (Job 7:21).

"But go thou thy way till the end be: for thou shalt rest, and stand in thy lot at the end of the days" (Dan. 12:13). "The end of the days" is when the angel shouts "that there should be time no longer" (Rev. 10:6). A person's "lot" in biblical terms is an appointed place. Daniel is not to stand in his appointed place until the end of days. His place will be in heaven once Christ returns and raises the righteous to life. Want some really solid evidence regarding death and the state of the dead?

Acts 2:29, 34 clearly explains the location of the dead. "Men and brethren, let me freely speak unto you of the patriarch David, that he is both dead and buried, and his sepulchre is with us unto this day.... *For David is not ascended into the heavens.*"

King David wrote, "For in death there is no remembrance of thee [God]: in the grave who shall give thee thanks?" (Ps. 6:5). If people went straight to heaven when they died, they would be praising God. But this text points to the fact that the dead are in the ground. Psalm 115:17 says something similar: "The dead praise not the Lord, neither any that go down into silence."

"His breath goeth forth, he returneth to his earth; in that very day *his thoughts perish*" (Ps. 146:4). If a person were in heaven, they would be able to think, but because they return to the dust, they don't know anything. "For the living know that they shall die: but the dead know not any thing ... Their love, and their hatred, and their envy, is now perished" (Eccl. 9:5, 6).

"And many of them that sleep in the dust of the earth shall awake, some to everlasting life, and some to shame and everlasting contempt" (Dan. 12:2). This verse indicates that everyone will awake to their reward or their punishment, but only at the appointed time.

John 5:28, 29 says, "Marvel not at this: for the hour is coming, in the which all that are in the graves shall hear his voice, and shall come forth; they that have done good, unto the resurrection of life; and they that have done evil, unto the resurrection of damnation." All, wicked and righteous, will hear Christ from *their graves,* not from heaven or hell. Although the righteous will hear that voice a thousand years before the wicked. Remember, the holy city descends after the thousand years and the wicked dead will be raised to their reward at that time.

The wisest man to ever live wrote this, "Whatsoever thy hand findeth to do, do it with thy might; for there is no work, nor device, nor knowledge, nor wisdom, in the grave, whither thou goest" (Eccl. 9:10).

"The Lord knoweth how to … reserve the unjust unto the day of judgment to be punished" (2 Peter 2:9). Notice they are not "punished" until "the day of judgment." This alone refutes the teaching that a person goes directly to a place of punishment at death.

In the next chapter of 2 Peter, we find these words: "But the heavens and the earth, which are now, by the same word [the same word which spoke all into creation] are kept in store, reserved unto fire against the day of judgment and perdition of ungodly men…. But the day of the Lord will come as a thief in the night; in the which the heavens shall pass away with a great noise, and the elements shall melt with fervent heat, the earth also and the works that are therein shall be burned up" (2 Peter 3:7, 10). It will literally be "hell on earth" when fire from heaven descends to consume the wicked (Rev. 20:9).

Then all things will be made new. "And I saw a new heaven and a new earth: for the first heaven and the first earth were passed away" (Rev. 21:1). Remember Shadrach, Meshach, and Abednego in the fiery furnace? Christ was with them in the furnace, and they weren't harmed, not even the smell of smoke was on them. So it will be in the New Jerusalem when the fire consumes those who compass the camp of the saints and sin is burned from the earth. The saints with Christ in the city will be safe, and the earth will be made new.

When Jesus raised Lazarus from the dead after four days in the grave, it was not some cruel trick to yank him from paradise, and Lazarus told no stories of being alive or awake elsewhere. Lazarus' sister Martha understood about the state of the dead, for she said, "I know that he shall rise again in the resurrection at the last day" (John 11:24). The *only* people the Bible mentions being in heaven (like Elijah, Enoch, or Moses) were specifically mentioned as being caught up or specially resurrected and taken to heaven.

I urge you to "incline your ear, come unto me: hear and your soul shall live" (Isa. 55:3). The truth about the state of the dead is clearly documented in the Bible.

The question must then arise that if the Bible does not teach that a person has a soul separate from the body, which violates the laws of judgment and reward by going to heaven or a non-existent hell, and the patriarchs and early Christians never taught such a thing, then where did it get started? Or when? We will examine the theory of the immortal soul in the next chapter according to history and the two common verses people use in support of the teaching of immortality.

Chapter 5

History of "Immortal Soul"

A lot of history exists here, but I'll be as brief as possible. Many great reformers such as Martin Luther recognized and taught against the "immortal soul" and modern day hell doctrine. Martin Luther even recognized its origins, but Calvinists kept it alive into modern Christianity, where Protestants kept it alive into the 1800s.

Amos Phelps (1805–1874), a Methodist in *Is Man by Nature Immortal?*, wrote, after extensive study, "This doctrine can be traced through the muddy channels of a corrupted Christianity, a perverted Judaism, a pagan philosophy, a superstitious idolatry, to the great instigator of mischief in the garden of Eden. The Protestants borrowed it from the Catholics, the Catholics from the Pharisees, the Pharisees from the Pagans, and the Pagans from the old Serpent, who first preached the doctrine amid the lowly bowers of Paradise to an audience all too willing to hear and heed the new and fascinating theology—'Ye shall not surely die.'"

Justin Martyr, a fixture and noted leader in the early churches founded by Jesus' disciples, had this to say before his death in AD 165: "If you have fallen in with some who are called Christians, but who do not admit this [the truth of the resurrection], and venture to blaspheme the God of Abraham, and the God of Isaac, and the God of Jacob; who say there is no resurrection of the dead, and that their souls, when they die, are taken to heaven; do not imagine that they are Christians" (*Dialogue with Trypho,* Chapter LXXX, Ante Nicene Father; 1:239).

You will notice how the doctrine first started with simply a soul going to heaven at death without the body and no resurrection. Later, this doctrine morphed in a kind of compromise to include a resurrection along with the false doctrine of a soul going directly to heaven. There was no word on how the two were expected to reunite, but it didn't take long for this to change further.

Tertullian (AD 160–225) further developed the doctrine to include "eternal torment," a phrase not found anywhere in the Bible, but introduced with his writings. He *theorized* that it must be the burning hell of Revelation and further that it must be a "renewing fire," which consumed and renewed a person as it burned. This doctrine seems to borrow principles from Persian dualism. If you read his works, you will discover that Tertullian's claims are all theories and are not backed up with any scriptural support. Furthermore, he made no claim that this was anything but a theory.

Later, Jerome and Augustine added to the new teaching, and it became an accepted "faith" of the Catholic Church. Those who refused to accept it were, by 1513, condemned to be burned at the stake or tortured to death. Then, on December 19, 1513, Pope Leo X declared the following in an official statement: "We do condemn and reprobate all who assert that the intelligent soul is mortal … all who adhere to the like erroneous assertions shall be shunned and punished as heretics."

This idea that the soul is immortal can also be found in Greek philosophy, Egyptian culture, Pantheism, and reincarnation, to name a few. Regardless of the variation of the philosophy, all of these ideas carry on the original lie told by Satan in Genesis 3:4, "Ye shall not surely die."

As these ideas infiltrated the church, Christians sought ways to justify the idea of immortality of the soul with the Bible. And they came up with two stories and a set of texts as their defense.

We will begin by looking at the parable of the rich man and Lazarus, which is found in Luke 16:19–31. The first thing to note is that this parable is just that, a parable. Let's not forget two important things about parables. First, they are not real; they are an illustration. Second, they had a purpose that was actually meant to confuse those who were unwilling to completely accept the truth. The reasons why Jesus spoke in parables are clearly stated in the Bible.

Matthew 13:34, 35 says, "All these things spake Jesus unto the multitude in parables; and without a parable spake he not unto them: that it might be fulfilled which was spoken by the prophet, saying, I will open my mouth in parables; I will utter things which have been kept secret from the foundation of the world." Now read Luke 8:10: "And [Jesus] said, Unto you it is given to know the mysteries of the kingdom of God: but to others in parables; that seeing they might not see, and hearing they might not understand."

Parables were a stumbling block for those who would consume the word in their lust for greed, power, and immature pursuits (such as the vengeful attitude of wanting to see people tortured for eons).

But was there another reason for this particular parable? Jesus spoke this parable directly to the Pharisees (Luke 15:2)—nowhere else was a parable spoken solely to one sect, or class, of people. Furthermore, Jesus called the Pharisees a generation of vipers (Matt. 3:7). Armed with this information, we can use these clues and a little bit of history to better understand what was going on here.

A study of Talmudic teachings and writings from the Sanhedrin, as well as other historical evidence outside Judaism, sheds some light. The Pharisees were the one Jewish sect who believed in the immortal soul. This was a pagan belief they had adopted from the Greeks. In their minds it was so irrefutable that any competent scholar wouldn't dare claim otherwise, at risk of academic suicide, or worse, being labeled a charlatan. In Acts 23:6–9 the apostle Paul actually used this belief to set the Pharisees and Sadducees against each other. Though Paul's upbringing was as a Pharisee, he did not adhere to their beliefs following his conversion to Christianity. It appears that Jesus used this illustration because it was something that would "hit home" with the Pharisees. Again, we must remember that this was a parable spoken to one specific sect.

As we examine the parable, we discover that it is not about hell. This a parable that foretells Jesus' resurrection and the simple truth that, as Jesus summed up, "If they hear not Moses and the prophets, neither will they be persuaded, though one rose from the dead" (Luke 16:31). The Pharisees, supposed scholars of Moses and the prophets, were not convinced of Jesus' deity, so how were they to believe on Him when He rose from the grave if they didn't believe on Him while on earth?

The parable illustrates their hopeless state if they continued in their refusal to accept the scriptures; they didn't believe the very words they claimed to so highly esteem! The Pharisees were the *only* ones connected with the Bible who were teaching the doctrine of an immortal soul, and they didn't believe Moses, Isaiah, David, Jeremiah, Micah, Ezekiel, Daniel, Zechariah, or Jesus. So should we trust their interpretation of scripture?

To be sure this is a parable, let's look at it in a realistic light. The fact remains that if any one part is figurative, the whole thing must be figurative; hence, it is a parable. The Bible always uses literalism and symbolism alone and does not mix the two in a single passage. Let's look at some of the specifics.

Abraham's bosom is not the home of the saved (see Hebrews 11:6, 10). This is figurative language. Because one went to Abraham's bosom and the other to hell, then the description of hell must also be figurative.

Those in heaven would not be able to speak with those in hell, nor will they even think of them (Isa. 65:17). All former things "are passed away" (Rev. 21:4).

The Bible teaches that the dead, good and bad, are in their graves (Job 17:3; 21:30–32), and they will hear Jesus' voice *from the grave* (John 5:28, 29).

The Bible clearly states that people receive their reward at Jesus' second coming, not at death (Rev. 22:11, 12; Matt. 16:27). Likewise, the dead are not punished at death, but after their judgment following the thousand years. Their punishment *is* death—the death penalty; "the second death." If the "wages of sin" were burning in hell, why is Jesus not burning in hell? He took our place and paid our penalty. He took the sins of the world upon Himself. "The soul that sinneth, it shall die" (Ezek. 18:20).

If taken literally, the parable would contradict the common teaching that a disembodied soul goes to hell (something this parable doesn't even suggest). The rich man is described with eyes, tongue, and lips. Notice, it was his body that was taken to hell. If you were to exhume a grave, you would see for yourself that the body is still there.

Tertullian and the others completely fabricated the idea of a disembodied soul with the thoughts and feelings of a human being. It is nowhere in the Bible. It is not even in the parable we just looked at. It's time to stop being a Pharisee and stumbling over this illustration.

Now let's examine the strongest argument for these teachings, one that I believed for some time. In defending the belief of immortality of the soul, many people point to the story of the thief on the cross.

Greek, what the New Testament was originally written in (with maybe the exception of Hebrews, which was written in both Greek and Hebrew), was the dominant language of the time. Few Jews outside of Jerusalem spoke Hebrew anymore. Greek is an inflected language, which means there is only one subject per sentence that can be modified, regardless of structure. The phrase "dog bites man" or "man bites dog" may be radically different in English, but in Greek, the meaning cannot get jumbled; the dog would still be doing the biting.

For example, have you ever heard of a sick handkerchief? "So that from his body were brought unto the sick handkerchiefs or aprons, and the diseases departed" (Acts 19:12). Oops. Someone misplaced a comma. The early English translators of the King James Version Bible added punctuation to the Bible since there weren't even chapter and verse divisions in the original writings.

Now let's look at the text in question. "And Jesus said unto him, Verily I say unto thee, today shalt thou be with me in paradise" (Luke 23:43). Written this way, it clearly impresses us with the idea that Jesus was to meet the thief that very day in heaven. But it creates a problem not only with the things we've studied, but with Jesus' statement to Mary when she found Him on the resurrection morning, "Touch me not; *for I am not yet ascended to my Father*: but go to my brethren, and say unto them, I ascend unto my Father, and your Father, and to my God and your God" (John 20:17). Jesus did not go to heaven until after His resurrection.

Something is either wrong, or we're missing something. Let's look at Luke 23:43 in the original Greek. This is what Jesus said to the thief on the cross: "AMEN SOI LEGO. SEMERON MET EMOU ESE EN TO PARADESO." Literal translation: "Truly to-you I-say today with-me you-will-be in the paradise." *Semeron* (today) is the adverb. Alone, it is impossible to know which it modifies: "I say" or "you-will-be." The "with-me" in this verse is *not a verb* and is not modified by the adverb "today." That would be illegal grammar. "With me" does belong to "you-will-be." Though no conclusive evidence can be made for any side of the debate, the scales tip in favor of the adverb modifying "I-say," whereas there is *no* support for the other rendering.

The bottom line is that when translating this verse into English it is not correct to say, "Today shalt thou be ..." The correct grammar would be, "today thou shalt be." The only question remains, where do we put the comma? There is enough evidence in the use of Greek to compel the following: "Verily I say unto thee today, thou shalt be with me in paradise." The adverb used here implies emphasis and this is the only usage that brings it into harmony. Jesus emphasizes that *today* He is promising the hope of the resurrection.

But, ultimately, when something is unclear and no definitive proof can be made, then neither should we use this to support our beliefs, nor should anyone else rely solely upon this verse for doctrine. And that is why I have devoted such time and effort into this study and this book. With all the evidence weighed together, I feel compelled to present this as fact and hope that others will see the justness and mercifulness of our God and dispense with the false teachings concerning hell and the unsaved.

Chapter 6

Danger of False Doctrine

The danger of false doctrines is threefold. First, and most obviously, it is a point by which many have rejected God, of whom the Bible claims is "just" and "fair" and "merciful" and who "is love" (see 1 John 4:8).

Second, many claim to be speaking with spirits of dead relatives, but in reality are being deceived by evil spirits. The Bible warns us of seducing spirits who will lead people astray in the last days. What false doctrine they will seek to impress upon their listeners we can but guess, but whatever they begin telling those who, through years of acceptance, have come to believe "spirits of the dead" to be either harmless, helpful, or good, it will lead to many people's destruction.

The fact is the Bible condemns consultation with what is termed "familiar spirits." God commanded that such mediums and people consulting these spirits be put to death (Lev. 20:27). God will destroy practitioners of these spiritism based "arts" when He returns. For a list of some which God calls an "abomination" see Deuteronomy 18:10–12.

The third danger has to do with confusion. In the book of Revelation we see Babylon take center stage. The word Babylon comes from "Babel," which literally means confusion. This originated at the Tower of Babel where God confused the languages in order to stop them from consolidating together for evil. "Therefore is the name of it called Babel; because the Lord did there confound the language of all the earth" (Gen. 11:9).

In the book of Revelation, Babylon is portrayed as a group of churches (a woman) that—without pulling any punches—Scripture calls a "whore." The "whore" mixes the "wine of her fornication" in a cup from which many drink (Rev. 17). This mixture is all the false and pagan doctrines adopted by the churches that will unite in the last days. Like wine, these teachings taste good, are intoxicating, and numb the mind. There is much to study in Revelation, but the basic teaching we are focusing on right now is that the whore represents impure churches and teachings. Thus, we must be careful.

Notice next that God calls out His people from all these churches. "And I heard another voice from heaven, saying, *Come out of her, my people,* that ye be not partakers of her sins, and that ye receive not of her plagues" (Rev. 18:4). Did you know that the word for church in Greek is *ekklesia*? That is the word used in the New Testament and used by the writers of those books. It literally means "called-out ones," which supports the Bible principle that the churches of Babylon are presenting false doctrines that God's true worshippers must abandon.

Notice also that God commands His people to come out. It is not an option, but a command. The time will come when it will no longer be safe to remain in those churches. Wine will have blinded many, and the plagues will be horrible. "In the cup which she hath filled fill to her double" (Rev. 18:6).

It is interesting to note that the seven last plagues to fall on the earth are seven of the ten that fell on Egypt before God brought His people out. Which seven? Hint: three fell on everyone, but seven fell on the Egyptians only.

As you can see, it is so important to study the Bible and understand prophecy as it points to the times we are living in.

Chapter 7

The Judgment

Now that we have discussed death and the resurrection, we need to wrap up this subject by examining the judgment. For many people this concept seems frightening. We've learned over the course of our lives that to be judged is to have someone nitpick every wrong we've done, in which case we're all doomed. But that is not the biblical standard for the judgment. The Bible teaches that judgment will be found in favor of the saints, those who confess Christ. "Judgment was made in favor of the saints of the Most High" (Dan. 7:22, NKJV).

Turn to Isaiah 11:3, 4: "And he shall not judge after the sight of his eyes, neither reprove after the hearing of his ears: But with righteousness shall he judge the poor, and reprove with equity for the meek of the earth." The poor and meek receive "with equity" their reward. Judgment doesn't just find the unrepentant guilty. Every court case has two sides: a winner and a loser. To announce judgment against one is to rule in favor of the other.

Peter wrote, "For the time is come that judgment must begin at the house of God: and if it first begin at us, what shall the end be of them that obey not the gospel of God?" (1 Peter 4:17).

Now let's read 2 Corinthians 5:10: "For we must all appear before the judgment seat of Christ; that every one may receive the things done in his body, according to that he hath done, whether it be good or bad."

When writing of the judgment, it is impossible to separate what we've studied in the previous chapters from our discussion here. Some things will be repeated, although we will be looking at completely new verses.

There are as many diverse teachings on Christ's judgment and return as there are religions. But are they biblical? Most believe their teachings are, but when analyzed using only the Bible, the doctrine usually fails to answer key questions and becomes quite contradictory. For years now, I've studied the tenets of different faiths, and I still read and dissect those teachings.

One of the more interesting statements I've seen concerning Christ's return has enormous implications concerning the judgment: "When Christ returns, He will initially have to *force* peace on humanity" (*The Good News,* November-December 2004, p. 7, emphasis in original). This statement, which appeared in *The Good News*, a free religious magazine, is not very well thought out. How do you "force" peace on anyone; the Bible teaches that this is a choice.

Now look at the United Church of God and the Philadelphia Church of God. They teach that after coming to earth and forcing His rule on the unwilling and slaughtering the rebellious "with a rod of iron," there will be 1,000 years of opportunity for people to accept Christ. But the Bible clearly, and in no uncertain terms, states that such teaching is apostasy. When Christ appears again, it will be "without sin unto salvation" (Heb. 9:28). The sacrifice is done. The sanctuary is cleansed (Heb. 8, 9). To claim that sinners will have the opportunity to put their own sins on Christ again, after He returns, would require Him to die once more on the cross.

The focus of this chapter then is to understand the atonement for sin and the judgment. The idea is not to put down anyone's beliefs, but to provide a balanced, scriptural approach for people to determine for themselves what is true. If you believe the things I write to be in error, you will at least have gained a scholarly position from which you can say, "I've read it, and this is where I believe he is wrong."

Earlier we read, "For the time is come that judgment must begin at the house of God: and if it first begin at us, what shall the end be of them that obey not the gospel of God?" (1 Peter 4:17). Even Christians go through a judgment.

The judgment, as can be determined from Scripture, is an investigative judgment. Why would an all-knowing God need to investigate, or expose, someone's "works" or hold such a trial to determine the saved and the lost? There are biblical examples where God asks questions and weighs evidence. The first such investigation occurred in the Garden of Eden when God asked, "Where are you?" "Who told you?" "Have you eaten from the tree?" "What is this you have done?" (see Gen. 3:9–13. After this investigation, judgment is pronounced (verses 14–19). Certainly God knew the answer to those questions, so why ask them?

There are two good reasons for an investigative judgment:

As in the garden, God's questioning brought awareness of the sin to the transgressor. In order for us to repent, we must first recognize our sin.

We must not forget that Satan first led one third of the heavenly host astray, claiming he could do it better and that God is unjust. There are other intelligent beings watching the outcome of this whole drama. This is also why God has allowed sin to run its course and has not yet destroyed Satan and the wicked. To do so when the arch deceiver first rebelled would have left people with the idea that maybe Satan was right and we had reason to fear God. Such is not true worship, but service born of fear. That is not God's way. Any teaching that states God will force Himself upon anyone is totally unfounded and completely unbiblical.

So, it is to be an investigative judgment. Read the parable of the wedding guests in Matthew 22:1–14. The king's inspection of the guests depicts who God will allow to enter into heaven. This story and so many others are for our benefit and that of the angelic beings.

When is the judgment going to take place? Revelation 14:7 tells us that the hour of judgment will come, but do we have a specific timeframe? "Fear God, and give glory to him; for the hour of his judgment is come" (Rev. 14:7). Before we get to the "when" more fully, we should explore the *system of* judgment and atonement.

The book of Hebrews in the New Testament spends a significant amount of time describing the sanctuary in heaven where Christ mediates as our High Priest. This sanctuary and mediation is the same as that of the tabernacle of the Old Testament. I strongly suggest reading Hebrews 8:1–6, 9:11–28 before going further. One of the key concepts to gain from these passages is that the tabernacle that was set up during the Exodus is an exact copy of the one in heaven. "We have such a high priest, who is set on the right hand of the throne of the Majesty in the heavens; a minister of the sanctuary, and of the *true tabernacle, which the Lord pitched, and not man*" (Heb. 8:1, 2, see also Heb. 9:11). This tabernacle is the one God had Moses copy: "As Moses was admonished of God when he was about to make the tabernacle: for, See, saith he, that thou make all things according to the pattern shewed to thee in the mount" (Heb. 8:5, see also Exod. 25:40; 26:30; and 27:8).

Hebrews 9:1–10 describes the ministration of that earthly tabernacle and tells us it was "a figure" (verse 9) of things to come. The blood sacrifice of Christ was the final culmination of all the "type and shadow" because "it is not possible that the blood of bulls and goats should take away sins" (Heb. 10:4). "It was therefore necessary that the patterns [the earthly tabernacle] of things in the heavens should be purified with these [bulls and goats]; but the heavenly things themselves with better sacrifices than these" (Heb. 9:23). And so, Christ's blood is offered in heaven: "Neither by the blood of goats and calves, but by his own blood he entered in *once* into the most holy place, having obtained eternal redemption for us" (Heb. 9:12).

Did you realize that we can look at the Old Testament sanctuary and its ministry to determine exactly what will occur at not only the judgment but also the end of the world? It was a "pattern," a "copy of the true" tabernacle in heaven.

Sacrifices for sins were offered daily. These sins accumulated and were transferred in ceremony to the Most Holy Place behind the second curtain where the ark of the covenant was kept. Once a year on the Day of Atonement the high priest entered into the Most Holy Place to "cleanse the sanctuary." The high priest wore bells and had a rope tied around his ankle. If the high priest had not confessed his sin or was defiled in some way, he would be immediately killed when he stepped foot in the Most Holy Place. Because anyone else entering the Most Holy Place would be killed, they used the bells to determine if the priest was alive, and the rope was to pull him out if he fell dead to the ground.

During the Day of Atonement the people fasted and "afflicted their souls" in prayer and supplication. They anxiously awaited the high priest's return, which signaled the assurance of

God's acceptance of their sacrificial offering. As soon as the high priest emerged from the Most Holy Place, he would bless the congregation.

So it will be with Christ. "So Christ was once offered to bear the sins of many; and unto them that look for him shall he *appear the second time without sin unto salvation*" (Heb. 9:28). We cannot miss this. When Christ appears again, sin is gone; the atonement is made; the sacrifice is over. The sacrifice is done once, and only once at the end of the world (Heb. 9:26). There is no second chance for anyone. "Now where remission of these is, there is no more offering for sin" (Heb. 10:18).

To give sinners a second chance would require Christ to be put on the cross again. "For then must he often have suffered since the foundation of the world: but now once in the end of the world hath he appeared to put away sin by the sacrifice of himself" (Heb. 9:26). Eternal destiny is decided when Christ leaves the heavenly sanctuary. It is impossible for there to be a second chance.

As we saw earlier, the wicked are destroyed by the brightness of His coming (2 Thess. 2:8). God does not leave people alive on this earth to procreate children into sin where no hope of salvation can be had. "And the slain of the Lord shall be at that day from one end of the earth unto the other end of the earth" (Jer. 25:33, see also Jer. 4:23–27). Jehovah's witnesses, at one time, taught that they would be spending months burying the bodies of the slain when Christ returns based on similar passages to that one. But we must read the rest of Jeremiah 25:33, which states, "they shall not be lamented, neither gathered, nor buried; they shall be dung upon the ground."

The Bible is clear that the sanctuary was cleansed, but where did the sin go? This is where it gets interesting. Once the sanctuary was cleansed and the offering accepted, the high priest placed his hand over a "scapegoat," transferring all of Israel's sins to it. The scapegoat, bearing all the accumulated sins for that year, was then sent "unto a land not inhabited" (Lev. 16:22). So it will be when Christ returns. Satan, the instigator of all sin, will bear not only the sins Christ bore on the cross but also his own for 1,000 years. God has a just plan. How can people burn for-ever when their sins are transferred to Satan? The wilderness he will be confined to is "the land [which] shall be utterly emptied" (Isa. 24:3), the earth in its desolate state. This is what is meant by Revelation 20:2, 3 when it says, "And he laid hold on the dragon, that old serpent, which is the Devil, and Satan, and bound him a thousand years, and cast him into the bottomless pit, and shut him up, and set a seal upon him, that he should deceive the nations no more." At this time Satan will be bound to the earth, unable to ascend to heaven or any other world.

The word used for bottomless pit is an "abyss," which is very similar to the Old Testament words meaning "without form and void." There can be no refuting this. In Genesis 1 the earth is described as being without form and void. In Jeremiah, concerning end-time prophecy, that phrase is used again to describe the earth after Christ's return. "I beheld the earth, and lo, it was without form, and void … the whole land shall be desolate" (Jer. 4:23, 27).

There is no reason to keep the wicked alive because they have made their choice. When Christ returns, probation is closed and the announcement is made: "He that is unjust, let him be unjust still: and he which is filthy, let him be filthy still: and he that is righteous, let him be righteous still: and he that is holy, let him be holy still. And, behold, I come quickly; and my reward is with me, to give every man according as his work shall be" (Rev. 22:11, 12).

Before we examine the prophecy of Daniel and the judgment going on now in the heavenly sanctuary, I want to discuss the danger of misleading doctrine concerning the judgment and Christ's return. We have nothing at all to fear by this judgment. Nothing. What we have to fear is being deceived into thinking that Christ is delaying His coming or that we can "get right with God" at the last minute or when He returns, but unfortunately, if we wait until then, it will be too late.

At the beginning of this chapter, I quoted a magazine article that teaches that Christ will "force" peace on humankind and reign on earth during the thousand years. Anyone familiar with the New Testament knows that Satan will eventually attempt to deceive the world into thinking he is Christ. Scripture makes it clear that before Jesus returns there must be a false Christ. How will he impersonate our Lord? What other way can there be but to pretend he is Christ returned again to reign here on earth?

"Let no man deceive you by any means: for that day shall not come, except there come a falling away first, and that man of sin be revealed, the son of perdition; who opposeth and exalteth himself above all that is called God, or that is worshipped; *so that he as God sitteth in the temple of God, shewing himself that he is God*" (2 Thess. 2:3, 4).

The Bible tells us that Satan masquerades as an "angel of light" (2 Cor. 11:14) and will seek to "deceive the very elect" if it were possible (Matt. 24:24). So how can we be safe from such powerful deception? Through knowing Scripture and relying on the true Word of God. The Bible tells us that Christ never touches the earth. When He returns, we will meet Him in the clouds (1 Thess. 4:17). Do you know what else Satan will try to do? He will claim to change one or more of God's commandments: "and he shall … think to change times and laws" (Dan. 7:25). Satan will seek to give credibility to the lie that the authority to change times and laws has been given to him. But God does not change (Mal. 3:6). And God's law is His character.

What can we learn about the "son of perdition" described in 2 Thessalonians 2:3, 4? There is only one person in all scripture who is called the "son of perdition"—Judas (John 17:12). It is reasonable that we should find some clues there.

As can easily be shown, Judas' motivation was not money—the thirty pieces of silver was a bonus he accepted because that is what the priests offered him for the betrayal of Jesus. Judas was a thief (John 12:6) with access to all kinds of money. He was profiting from Christ's presence far more than he would from Jesus' imprisonment or death. Judas wanted that to continue with one added benefit—power.

Judas saw Christ's miracles and witnessed His escape many times. Judas *knew* Christ was the Messiah. Jesus didn't call Judas like the rest; Judas attached himself to Christ's discipleship. So why did he do it? I'm sure Judas thought it pure genius, but he wasn't the first to think that way. "Then those men, when they had seen the miracle that Jesus did, said, This is of a truth that prophet that should come into the world. When Jesus therefore perceived that they would come and take him by force, to make him a king, he departed again into a mountain himself alone" (John 6:14, 15).

Many Jews were expecting the Messiah, at His coming, to reign on earth, overthrow other nations, and rule them with a "rod of iron" (Ps. 2:9). But Jesus said, "My kingdom is not of this world" (John 18:36).

Judas reasoned that if he could force Christ to use His power on the rulers and priests to free Himself His kingship would be all but established. Judas, the money holder/disciple, figured that he would then gain immense position and power. Judas most likely believed he was doing the right thing and, regardless of motivation, was helping fulfill prophecy. Christ's words on the night of betrayal must have sounded like a blessing, "That thou doest, do quickly" (John 13:27). And here we find a solemn warning: people who turn Christ's words into sanction for their actions but put *their* designs ahead of God's will come to the point where they can no longer discern truth from error.

Judas misunderstood a fundamental truth about God. He does not force Himself upon anyone. Worship in fear is no worship at all. We should follow Christ based on a simple, trusting love of righteousness by faith. God lets people simply accept or reject Him. Did you know that God doesn't decide who is worthy of salvation? He deems everyone worthy of His kingdom. We judge ourselves and decide our own fate: "Then Paul and Barnabas waxed bold, and said, It was necessary that the word of God should first have been spoken to you: but seeing ye put it from you, and *judge yourselves unworthy of everlasting life,* lo, we turn to the Gentiles" (Acts 13:46).

In the Dark Ages the Roman papacy committed its atrocities based upon a theological justification entwined with a single verse of Luke 14:23: "compel them to come in."

So when the United Church of God declares, "when Christ returns He will initially have to *force* peace on humanity" (emphasis theirs) and will rule with a rod of iron and slaughter millions in unrepentant nations, they are building the same historical foundation for the torture and murder of those who refused to believe the papacy in the Dark Ages. They will believe the son of perdition when he claims to be Christ and calls for the enforcement of his laws under threat of punishment.

Their atrocities are foretold in Scripture. "They shall put you out of the synagogues: yea, the time cometh, that whosoever killeth you will think that he doeth God service. And these things will they do unto you, because they have not known the Father, nor me" (John 16:2, 3). Did you catch that the part about knowing the Father? We need to *know* the character of God or we are on perilous ground. Scripture tells us He is love. Nowhere can we find where God has forced people to worship Him as Nebuchadnezzar attempted with Shadrach, Meshach, and Abednego. History has always shown (with frightening "hindsight") that true Christians were killed by those calling them heretics and claiming to do so in the name of the Lord.

Although the time prophecies of Daniel deserve their own book, I will do my best to outline them in relation to their importance to the investigative judgment. The book of Daniel contains more than 2,000 years of historical events (prophesied before they occurred) in such flawless and chronological detail it has left many scholars stunned.

The longest time prophecy given in Daniel is this: "Unto two thousand and three hundred days; then shall the sanctuary be cleansed" (Dan. 8:14). This is the overall timeline from which the rest in that book are but portions. You could think of the book as an outline of 2,300 years with segments broken down in different chapters. What must be understood is this: (1) the book of Daniel and Revelation coincide; and (2) when dealing with prophecy, days represent years, as proven in Scripture.

For Israel's transgression in the wilderness, God assigned a day for a year to be spent wandering in the desert. "After the number of the days in which ye searched the land, even forty days, each day for a year, shall ye bear your iniquities, even forty years" (Num. 14:34). God appointed Ezekiel, during the Babylonian exile (which Daniel was a part of and where that book was written), the same day for a year principle (Ezek. 4:4–13)—"I have appointed thee each day for a year" (verse 6). There has been no serious dispute concerning the principle of a day for a year in biblical prophecy—2,300 days simply means 2,300 years. The important thing to remember is that the Jewish calendar contained 360 days in a year (30 days per month).

Before you jump to conclusions and assume the 2,300 year prophecy means Christ should have returned hundreds of years ago, we must first realize two things. We have to know when that date begins, which the Bible tells us, and we also must remember that no one knows the exact day of the Lord's return. What we learn from the 2,300-year prophecy is that at the end of the 2,300 years, which occurred in 1844, the cleansing of the sanctuary in heaven began. This marks the point at which Jesus, our High Priest, entered the Most Holy Place in heaven and began His work of judging each person in the world. The dead are judged first, then those who are alive to determine who will go to heaven with Christ when He returns. So where are we in this judgment? No one knows. But so many prophecies in Matthew, Luke, and Revelation have already been fulfilled that we are nearing the end of this world as we know it.

Let's look at a few specifics in Daniel, which take us from early world history to the great reformation of the 1840s.

"But thou, O Daniel, shut up the words, and seal the book, even to the time of the end: many shall run to and fro, and knowledge shall be increased" (Dan. 12:4). The time of the end began in 1798 with the capture of the Catholic pope by General Berthier of Napoleon's army. At that point the book was no longer sealed—it could now be understood by the revealing of the prophecies within its pages. Think about the explosion of knowledge since then.

Now read Daniel 7:24, 25: "And the ten horns out of this kingdom [Rome] are ten kings that shall arise: and another shall arise after them; and he shall be diverse from the first, and he shall subdue three kings. And he shall speak great words against the most High, and shall wear out the saints of the most High, and think to change times and laws: and they shall be given into his hand until a time and times and the dividing of time." Literally, this means three and a half years. This equals 1,260 days. We see this number repeated throughout Revelation.

In Revelation 13 we find almost word for word the same passages found here. We also find the time forty-two months, which, at thirty days per month, is again 1,260 days. "And there was given unto him a mouth speaking great things and blasphemies; and power was given unto him to continue forty and two months … and it was given unto him to make war with the saints, and to overcome them" (Rev. 13:5, 7). The beasts in this chapter are the same found in Daniel. See also Revelation 11:2 and 12:6 where it is specifically called 1,260 days.

The three kingdoms plucked up by the religious/political power, the papacy and her armies, from the ten are the Ostrogoths, the Visigoths, and the Heruli. When the last were destroyed, the Vatican received her seat and authority by decree in AD 538. When General Berthier of Napoleons' army took the pope captive to France in 1798, where he immediately died, the papacy was dissolved. Exactly 1,260 years had expired. Years filled with the blood of—by conservative historical estimates—fifty million men, women, and children. But Revelation 13 continues where Daniel does not, stating twice that the "deadly wound was healed" (verses 3 and 12). In 1929 the Latin treaty restored the Vatican to power and the newspaper headlines declared, in eerie prophetic pronouncement, "deadly wound healed."

If we read Revelation 10:10, we discover "the little book" that was "sweet as honey" but after "eaten" was bitter. At the first, the words were sweet, but soon bitter disappointment reigned. Unlike Daniel, the book of Revelation was never sealed. "And he saith unto me, Seal not the sayings of the prophecy of this book: for the time is at hand" (Rev. 22:10). The book of Revelation is meant to be understood. Let's return to our 2,300-year outline that takes us to the year 1844.

In Daniel 8 he has a vision that culminates in the cleansing of the sanctuary (verse 14). The subsequent verses are an explanation by the angel Gabriel, in plain language, of the meaning of that vision. In verse 16 Gabriel is told to make Daniel understand the vision, but as verse 27 declares, Daniel became sick and fainted, undoubtedly because of the horrific things he witnessed over that 2,300 year period of time. Daniel plainly states in verse 27 that he did not understand, so Gabriel's charge is not yet complete. When Daniel is capable, Gabriel was to complete his mission. This occurs in the next chapter, although a period of nearly a year elapsed.

Daniel is praying for Jerusalem (Dan. 9:1–19) when Gabriel returns. The angel answers two questions here; neither of which Daniel had been praying for. There is seventy years of desolation, which is just about ended. This is not part of Daniel's prophecy. The seventy weeks (or 490 years) mentioned in the following verses concern Christ's coming. The key to understanding the 2,300 years lies right here in this prophecy. Gabriel has returned to finish explaining the vision, and here he begins breaking it down into segments.

"Seventy weeks are determined upon thy people and upon thy holy city" (Dan. 9:24). The word here translated as "determined" means cut out like a portion (or slice of pie), set aside from a whole. Four hundred and ninety years will be determined from the 2,300 years (begun in chapter 8) for Israel. This portion is at the beginning of the prophecy and so, if we determine the start date of one, we have the date for the other. "Know therefore and understand, that from the going forth of the commandment to restore and to build Jerusalem unto the Messiah the Prince shall be seven weeks, and threescore and two weeks" (Dan. 9:25). The decree that restored the government of Jerusalem and authorized a complete rebuilding of the city and its walls was issued by Artaxerxes in the autumn of 457 BC. With this decree many exiles returned to Israel. Twenty three hundred years takes us down through time to the cleansing of the sanctuary, which begins in 1844.

A great reformation took place around 1840, when many around the world heralded the soon return of Christ based on the prophecies of Daniel and Revelation, which were finally being understood. But they were in for a bitter disappointment, just as Revelation foretold. When 1844 rolled by and Jesus did not appear, many left the Christian faith, proving that their hearts were not sincere.

"And the voice which I heard from heaven spake unto me again, and said, Go and take the little book which is open in the hand of the angel which standeth upon the earth. And I went unto the angel, and said unto him, Give me the little book. And he said unto me, Take it, and eat it up; and it shall make thy belly bitter, but it shall be in the mouth sweet as honey" (Rev. 10:8). The little book was the book of Daniel. People ate up those words, and in the mouth of those who preached its message, the return of Christ was sweet. But the bitter disappointment, which left their stomach in knots with uncertainty, soon followed.

There disappointment stemmed from the misunderstanding of one thing: the sanctuary spoken of is in heaven and the cleansing marked the point when the judgment began. As Revelation states, "the hour of his judgment is come" (Rev. 14:7). Sadly, the message was all but lost after the disappointment. But there is a call to heed the messages of the three angels in Revelations 14 who are charged with spreading this message in the last days along with two other messages. The time has come to prepare for Christ's return.

"Then shall the kingdom of heaven be likened unto ten virgins, which took their lamps, and went forth to meet the bridegroom.… While the bridegroom tarried, they all slumbered and slept. And at midnight there was a cry made, Behold, the bridegroom cometh; go ye out to meet him.… And the foolish said unto the wise, Give us of your oil; for our lamps are gone out" (Matt. 25:1–8).

If we are to be ready for the Bridegroom when He returns, we must ask the Holy Spirit to guide us. Christ is in the heavenly sanctuary judging the world, and He will soon return to take to heaven with Him those who have accepted Him as their Savior. If we are to commit ourselves to following what is true, we must ask Jesus into our hearts and let the Holy Spirit fill us and lead us into all truths.

We have barely scratched the surface of the important prophecies found in Daniel and Revelation. However, I hope this information has generated a desire for the truth and will propel you forward into further study. For a detailed verse-by-verse study of Daniel and Revelation, I recommend *Daniel and the Revelation* by Uriah Smith, a remarkable author who came out of the great reformation. In his book Uriah Smith lists all the historical fulfillments of the events in Daniel, giving dates, names, and locations.

May God bless you as you study His Word and seek to follow the clear truths that are set before us in Scripture.

We invite you to view the complete
selection of titles we publish at:

www.TEACHServices.com

Scan with your mobile
device to go directly
to our website.

Please write or email us your praises, reactions, or
thoughts about this or any other book we publish at:

TEACH Services, Inc.
P U B L I S H I N G

www.TEACHServices.com • (800) 367-1844

P.O. Box 954
Ringgold, GA 30736

info@TEACHServices.com

TEACH Services, Inc., titles may be purchased in bulk for
educational, business, fund-raising, or sales promotional use.
For information, please e-mail:

BulkSales@TEACHServices.com

Finally, if you are interested in seeing
your own book in print, please contact us at

publishing@TEACHServices.com

We would be happy to review your manuscript for free.